WHY, WHAT, HOW

The Step-by-Step Playbook for Creating a Memorable Brand

Stephen Marinaro

Why, What, How:
The Step-by-Step Playbook for Creating a Memorable Brand

Paperback ISBN: 979-8-89576-072-7
Hardback ISBN: 979-8-89576-073-4

Published by:

AUTHORS on MISSION

Table of Contents

Introduction

My name is Stephen Marinaro, but most people know me as TheSalonGuy®. Over the last 30 years in the professional salon industry, I've learned exactly what it takes to build a real, lasting brand. But this isn't just about the beauty industry—it's about helping *you* build a personal brand that drives real results, no matter your field. Whether you're an entrepreneur, freelancer, or professional looking to grow your clientele and business, this book will give you the tools to create an authentic online presence that connects and converts.

Let me be direct about my credibility: it's in the results. Over 1 million YouTube subscribers, TikTok videos hitting 29 million views, national TV appearances, and a 7-figure hair care brand. For over 15 years, I've been creating content and building my brand—you may have read about me in Gary Vaynerchuk's *Crushing It*, caught one of my hair tutorials on YouTube, or even seen me on TV.

But here's what really matters: I'm still in the trenches every day, still creating, still building. I'm not just talking about it; I'm doing it.

I've spent thousands on books, courses, and programs—you probably have, too. And how many times have you gotten two hours into a book, only to feel like you're stuck in endless stories and meaningless theory? This book is different. Think of it as your tactical handbook: no fluff, no long-winded stories—just the essential information you need to get results *fast*.

My approach is unique. Before diving full-time into content creation, I spent six years as a firefighter and in law enforcement, leaving the field after 9/11. Even then, I was still doing hair on the side—it's in my blood. But those years taught me something invaluable: tactical procedures save lives. I've taken that same precise, strategic mindset and applied it to building a brand. I know what it means to build something from scratch.

Throughout this book, three simple icons mark the core concepts we'll cover, giving you a clear, actionable roadmap to success. Whether you're just starting, looking to scale, or an established brand stuck in a rut, there's something for everyone.

WHY	WHAT	HOW
The Purpose	The Plan	The Execution
Why do it?	What will you do?	How will you do it?

Let's get real. Ninety percent of people talk about making changes for years but never do anything. Almost everyone has a dream, but few do anything to make it a reality. If you're looking for another book to sit on your shelf while you "think about it," stop reading now. This book is for action-takers.

My personal journey started 15 years ago during one of the most trying times in my life—when my mother was sick and then passed. I took her strength and courage and used it as fuel to turn my own dream into reality. "Failure is not an option" became more than just words to me; it became my way of life.

As you embark on your own business journey, there are going to be those moments when you want to give up. That's when you need to keep going.

Trust me, I've been there. I remember walking 20 blocks in the pouring rain through Manhattan in a suit and tie, lugging bags of camera gear, killing my feet just to film some videos. And I just kept asking myself, "Is this worth it?"

Yes. But only because I have never given up.

This book is a roadmap for *you* to actually build something real—not a scam, or a "get rich quick" scheme, or even fake promises. Just tactics that really work. I'll provide you with the strategies and tools that I used to get started and that I continue to use today to continue to grow my brand to new heights. I had to develop my own blueprint for success, with lots of trial and error along the way.

I'm so confident that my method can be applied to building a brand in any industry that I've put everything that works for me together in one place to help take the guesswork out of it for others. You'll find worksheets, exercises, and examples to help you focus on what you want your brand to look like and how to help it grow.

The book is divided into three sections, each focusing on one of three critical questions that changed my life and could do the same for yours:

1. **WHY** do you want to build this brand?
2. **WHAT** are you going to do?
3. **HOW** are you going to do it?

Ready to get started? Let's do this.

FOLLOW

Follow @thesalonguy on all social media platforms

To purchase hair care products on Shopify:
shop.thesalonguy.com

To purchase courses: courses.thesalonguy.com

YouTube: youtube.com/thesalonguy

Section 1: The WHY

My WHY: *Helping other stylists build successful careers while giving clients the knowledge they deserve.*

Your WHY is what gives your brand a soul. It's bigger than making money; it is about creating something meaningful people can connect with on a deeper level.

I started creating content while my mother was fighting her illness. Seeing her strength in those moments helped me find my WHY. It wasn't about being famous or making money. It was about respecting her courage by helping others build something for themselves. That's what motivates me daily.

Use this QR code to watch an emotional and powerful video where I share how my mother's strength during her final days became the driving force behind everything I do.

Watch as I explain how personal experiences, even difficult ones, can become the fuel that powers your purpose and helps you discover your true WHY.

Finding your WHY often comes from your deepest life experiences. So, let me be clear: if you're only in this for the money, you won't last. I've seen so many people jump into content creation, thinking it's a get-rich-quick scheme. They post a few videos, don't get instant success, and quit.

Why? Because they had no real purpose driving them.

Your WHY gets you through the tough times. It's what pushed me to keep going while filming videos in the rain, editing until 3 a.m., and wondering if anyone would ever watch. Money can't fuel that kind of dedication. Only purpose can.

Think about it like this: When I started TheSalonGuy®, I could have just been some other hairstylist who does random videos. Instead, I focused on my why: helping other stylists build successful careers while giving clients the knowledge they deserve. That purpose drove everything: what I created, how I created it, and my entire brand.

Let's get down to business and find your WHY—not some fluffy mission statement, but your real, core purpose—the thing that will keep you going when motivation fades and obstacles seem overwhelming.

We'll cover:

- How to discover your true purpose
- How having a strong WHY prevents burnout
- How to turn your WHY into a brand mission
- The warning signs of a weak WHY
- How to build and strengthen your WHY

Your WHY is waiting. Not in some complicated business theory, but in your gut, your heart, your experience. These next chapters will help you find it, define it, and transform it into the foundation of a brand that lasts.

QUICK START GUIDE: THE WHY ACCELERATOR

Want to skip the theory and jump right into action? This is your tactical roadmap for finding your WHY in just 60 minutes. Think of it as your rapid-deployment strategy—the bare minimum you need to get started right now. This turbo-approach will get you moving quickly, but it is not a substitute for reading the chapters in detail. The content of each chapter provides deeper insights that will fortify your foundation. For now, take out a timer, find a quiet space and let's build your WHY.

Quick Start Guide to Finding Your WHY
60-Minute Action Plan
15 Minutes: Write your origin story • What made you start your brand? • What problem frustrated you most that you wanted to solve?
15 Minutes: List your proof points • What have you accomplished? • Which problems have you successfully solved?
15 Minutes: Define your target audience • Who needs your help? Be specific. • How will you change their life?
15 Minutes: Create your WHY statement **Use the format:** I help (specific group) achieve (specific result) by (your unique reason).

Red Flags Checklist
• Is money your only motivation?
• Do you change focus or direction every few weeks?
• Would you quit if success took five years to achieve?

Quick Test Your WHY

- Can you explain it in one sentence?
- Does it solve a real problem?
- Would you do it even if you weren't paid?
- Does it excite you to talk about it and to share with others?

Chapter 1: The Power of WHY

Your WHY isn't just a nice idea. It's the engine that drives everything you do.

Let's start with a simple truth: purpose is the reason behind your actions. Without it, you're just another person posting content or selling products.

TheSalonGuy® Story

When I started in the hair industry, I didn't just want to cut hair. I wanted to educate, inspire, and help others succeed. That deeper purpose pushed me to build courses, launch products like Tidal Wave, and create content for TheSalonGuy® YouTube channel. I didn't chase trends. I created a brand that aligned with my purpose of helping people feel more confident and successful.

Why do you want to build your brand?

Before you build your brand strategy, much less craft content, it's important to understand what fuels your fire. For me, it was my mom's strength and the will to help others succeed.

 For you, that might be family, financial freedom, or simply wanting to solve some problem facing your industry.

Whatever that is, it will be your fuel.

The Impact of Purpose

Without Clear Purpose

- Jumps on every trend, lacking uniqueness
- Content feels fake and inauthentic
- Quick burnout from chasing metrics

With Clear Purpose

- Clear content strategy and focus
- Authentic content that resonates
- Loyal community that believes in your brand

When your purpose is defined, your content transforms from scattered and disconnected to focused, authentic, and impactful. This change has ripple effects that affect every part of your strategy, from how your audience engages with you to how you'll sustain success in the long run.

TheSalonGuy® Story

Here's a real example. When I was starting out, everyone was doing quick viral trends. I could have joined in, but instead, I focused on creating detailed hair tutorials and educational content. It took longer to grow, but I built something real. Now, years later, while trend-chasers have come and gone, my audience stays loyal because they know exactly what I stand for.

Finding Your Mission

Your personal mission and brand mission must align. Every piece of content, product, and course I create ties back to my core purpose: helping others succeed in the beauty industry.

Here's how to develop a mission that works:

- **Make It Personal**
    - What frustrates you about your industry?
    - What problems do you wish someone had solved for you?
    - What change do you want to create?

- **Make It Practical**
    - How can you actually help people?
    - What specific solutions can you offer?
    - What unique perspective do you bring?

- **Make It Profitable**
    - How does your purpose solve real problems?
    - What value can you create for others?
    - How can you turn your mission into sustainable income?

- **Make It Clear**
    - Can you explain your mission in one sentence?
    - Would your target audience immediately understand it?
    - Does it guide your business decisions?

Every business choice I make stems from my mission. Whether it's introducing a product, partnering with others, or creating content, I ask: Will this further my goal of educating and empowering those in the beauty industry?

Take Action: Find Your Purpose

Authenticity, not perfection, defines your purpose.

 A clear WHY transforms your work, bringing clarity to your content, strength to your message, and depth to your influence. Creating videos or products is easy, but a brand that endures is built on purpose.

The next chapter will guide you to discover your WHY, but for now, use these exercises to lay the foundation for what's ahead.

1. **Write Your Purpose Statement**
   o Example: "I want to help hairstylists master their craft and build successful businesses."

2. **List Your Solutions**
   o What problems do you see that you can fix? Write them all down.

3. **Reality Check**
   o Be clear on what is a "passion" and what you can actually earn income from. It's the WHY behind it. Can you make this a career? Can you make money from it? If yes, you're good to go!

4. **Share your purpose with someone you trust.**
   o If it doesn't feel authentic, keep refining it.

5. **Test Your Mission**
   o Can you explain it in 30 seconds?
   o Does it excite you when you talk about it?
   o Would you pursue it even if money wasn't involved?

Chapter 2:
Finding Your WHY is Critical

Why Finding Your WHY Is Critical

If you don't have a clear reason behind your work, how will your audience find one to support you? If you don't know why you're creating, neither will they. Your WHY brings focus and clarity to decisions, giving your brand purpose.

TheSalonGuy® Story

When I created TheSalonGuy®, my WHY was crystal clear: I wanted to give back to the hair industry that had helped me succeed. That purpose informed every piece of content, product, and decision. That clarity helped me endure countless nights of editing and days of zero engagement. I knew exactly why I was doing this, even when no one was watching.

How to Discover Your WHY

Let's break this down into practical steps:

1. **Reflect on Your Personal Story**
   - Ask yourself:
     - What challenges have you overcome?
     - What lessons shaped your life and career?
     - What moments made you who you are?

2. **Identify Your Passions and Strengths**
   - Your WHY often lives where your talents meet your passion.
   - Ask yourself:

- What could you talk about for hours without getting bored?
- What are you known for among friends and peers?
- What skills come naturally to you?

3. **Understand Who You Want to Help**
   - Ask yourself:
     - Who are you really trying to reach?
     - What problems can you solve for them?
     - How can you make their lives better?

4. **Think About Legacy**
   - This is bigger than likes or followers.
   - Ask yourself:
     - What do you want to be remembered for?
     - How do you want to impact your industry?
     - What change do you want to create?

TheSalonGuy® Story

I realized I had a gift for explaining complex hairstyling techniques in simple ways. Combining that with my passion for helping others succeed, that's where I found my WHY. It wasn't just about doing hair anymore; it was about empowering others to build their own success stories.

Going back to Chapter 1, true *purpose* is what drives connection and inspires trust, paving the way for lasting success.

Making Your WHY Real

Let's cut through the fluff and get straight to making your WHY real. Here's my step-by-step process, which has worked for me and thousands of others I've helped build their brands.

A 3-Step Guide to Finding Your WHY

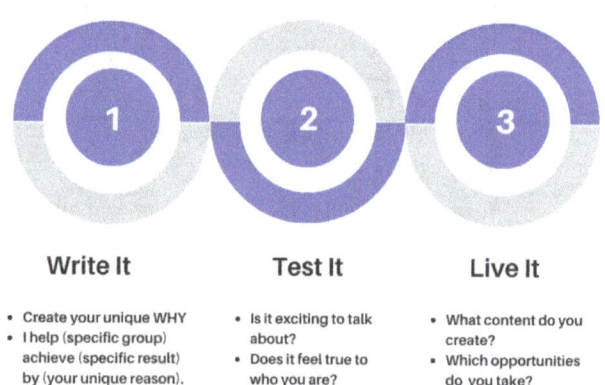

Write It

- Create your unique WHY
- I help (specific group) achieve (specific result) by (your unique reason).

Test It

- Is it exciting to talk about?
- Does it feel true to who you are?
- Would you still do it if you were rich?

Live It

- What content do you create?
- Which opportunities do you take?
- How do you communicate?

Many people overcomplicate this. They think achieving their goals requires some deep philosophical journey or fancy business framework. It doesn't. Your WHY is probably staring you right in the face; you just need to recognize it.

TheSalonGuy® Story

Whenever I launch a product like Tidal Wave or create a new course, I ask myself: *Does this align with my WHY of helping others succeed?* If the answer isn't a clear yes, I don't do it. It's that simple. That's why my audience trusts me. They know I'm not just trying to make a quick buck.

Take Action

Your WHY isn't set in stone from the start.

 It evolves and gains clarity, but its core should feel deeply personal. If you're trying too hard to impress, you're likely missing the mark. Take your time to uncover what feels genuine and aligned with who you are.

Next, we'll talk about how to strengthen your WHY and avoid the common pitfalls that can weaken it. But first, take the time to complete these exercises. They are the foundation for everything you will build. You have already started thinking about your story, passion, and impact statement in previous exercises. Here, I ask you to go deeper, adding or refining details.

1. **Your Story**
   - Write down your top three life-changing moments. What did they teach you?

2. **Your Passion List**
   - Create three columns:
     - What you're good at
     - What you love doing
     - What problems you can solve
   - Look for where they intersect

3. **Your Impact Statement**
   - Complete this sentence:
   - "I want to help _____ achieve _____ because _____."

4. **Reality Test**
   - Share your WHY with three people you know well.
   - Ask them: "Does this sound like me?"

Chapter 3: Building a Strong WHY

To be blunt: A weak WHY can destroy your brand faster than any change in algorithms or shifts in the market. I've seen it time and again. People with real potential walk away, not because they lack ability, but because their WHY wasn't strong enough to carry them through tough times. It's heartbreaking, but true. Your WHY must be powerful enough to push you forward.

A Weak WHY Is a Brand Killer

Consider your WHY as the guiding force behind your actions. Without it, you're simply wandering aimlessly.

- Your content jumps from trend to trend with no real direction
- Your message changes daily because you're chasing what's popular
- Your audience can't connect because they don't know your purpose
- Every setback hits harder; you have no deeper purpose pushing you

---

TheSalonGuy® Story

When I launched TheSalonGuy®, I was laser-focused on my WHY. I wasn't chasing fame or money. I wanted to share my knowledge and experience to help others grow. There were difficult moments when views were low, and sales were slow, but I kept going. That's what allowed me to build successful products, launch HairAdvisor, and create educational content that hairstylists rely on today.

Warning Signs Your WHY Needs Work

We must be clear on warning signs. These might seem like small problems, but they're actually red flags that your WHY is off track. I watch creators brush these aside all the time, assuming they'll resolve things later. By the time they realize it, their brand is often already in trouble.

Here are the four biggest red flags I've noticed time and time again:

- **You Keep Changing Directions**
  - One day, you're a lifestyle creator, the next, you're selling courses on a completely unrelated topic
  - Your content has no consistent theme or message
  - You chase every new platform or trend

- **Money Is Your Only Driver**
  - You promote anything that pays, regardless of value
  - Your audience feels like ATMs, not people
  - Every post is trying to sell something

- **You're Burning Out Fast**
  - Creating content feels like a chore
  - You're always comparing yourself to others
  - Small setbacks make you want to quit

- **Your Audience Isn't Sticking Around**
  - High follower churn
  - Low engagement
  - Comments are shallow or spam

 Use this QR code to listen to me detail the warning signs that your WHY needs strengthening.

Learn how to identify the dangerous distractions of chasing materialistic goals, losing focus, and jumping between pursuits.

The earlier you understand these warning signs, the better equipped you will be to avoid wasting your time and energy on a shaky foundation.

THE WRONG WHY (AND WHY IT FAILS)

Surface-level motivations don't sustain long-term success

Fame	Money	Trends
"I want to be famous."	"I want to get rich quick."	"I want in on the most popular trends."
Fame is temporary and fickle. Purpose lasts.	Money follows value. Focus on the value of your brand first.	Trends come and go. Focus on what's sustainable and aligns with your identity.

Don't freak out if any of these signs appear in your business. They're not a death sentence for your brand but a wake-up call. The good news is that you can fix all of these issues by revisiting and strengthening your WHY.

Building a Stronger WHY

Now that you know the warning signs, let's fix them. Strengthening your WHY starts with getting clear on what truly motivates you and making sure every action you take aligns with that drive.

Here's the step-by-step process to make your WHY stronger:

- **Stop and Reflect**
  - Take a hard look at what you're doing and why
  - Be honest about your real motivations
  - Strip away the ego and status-seeking

- **Simplify Your Mission**
  - What problem are you actually solving?
  - Who are you really helping?
  - Can you explain it to a 10-year-old?

- **Communicate It Clearly**
  - Your audience should understand your WHY instantly
  - Every piece of content should reflect it
  - Your products/services should support it

- **Rebuild with Purpose**
  - Align everything with your WHY
  - Cut anything that doesn't serve your mission
  - Stay consistent with your message

Strengthening your WHY is an ongoing process. As your brand evolves, you'll continue refining it. Each time you do, your brand becomes more resilient. Your content improves, and your audience becomes more engaged.

Take Action: Strengthen Your WHY

 Your WHY is the core of everything you build. When you get this right, everything else becomes much easier.

So, ensure your foundation is solid. No shortcuts here.

In the next section, we'll move to the WHAT: turning your strong WHY into actionable content and offerings. But first, ensure your foundation is firm. Take time with these exercises.

1. **Write a New WHY Statement**
   o   Keep it under 15 words
   o   Focus on impact, not income
   o   Make it something you'd be proud to share

2. **Audit Your Brand**
   o   Review your last 10 posts
   o   Check your product descriptions
   o   Read your bio on every platform
   o   Do they all reflect your WHY?

3. **Create Purpose-Driven Content**
   o   Plan your next 5 pieces of content
   o   Each should clearly connect to your WHY
   o   Share the purpose behind what you do

This exercise shouldn't be a one-time activity. Consider returning to it quarterly to keep on track.

Zero to Launch:
Your First 24 Hours of WHY

This 24-hour Launch Plan and First Week Schedule provide a clear roadmap to help you confidently transition from planning to execution.

Whether you're launching your brand for the first time or already have a brand identity, this 24-hour Launch Plan applies to you. It is the blueprint for moving forward with your brand now that you've defined or *redefined* your WHY. Whether you're a professional in the hair industry, an aspiring creator, or an entrepreneur, these timelines are designed to simplify the process and get you moving forward without hesitation.

Launch Plan
First 24-Hours
Hours 1-2: Brainstorm your expertise • List everything you know and are good at • Circle your top 3 skills
Hours 3-4: Plan your content • Choose 1 platform • Plan 5 pieces of content
Hours 5-6: Create your first piece of content • Film or write 1 piece • Keep it under 5 minutes/less than 1 page
Hours 7-8: Set up an online presence • Create or update your bio to include your WHY • Link to one piece of content

Week 1 Schedule
Monday: Film or Write Content **Tuesday:** Edit and Polish Content **Wednesday:** Post Content and Engage with Audience **Thursday:** Assess Engagement and Learn from Feedback **Friday:** Plan Next Week's Content

Following this guide, you'll create your initial content, establish a presence, and build sustainable routines in just one week. Don't wait for ideal circumstances. Set your 24-hour clock and begin your launch today. In my own business, this launch plan might look something like the following:

1. **Brainstorm content ideas.** See what is trending, popular or what viewers are asking for. Perhaps a new popular cut or trend fits my brand and would be something my audience would like.

2. **Confirm if the content theme will resonate with a broader audience.** This helps me not isolate and diminish my potential. If possible, create 5 separate pieces of content revolving around this idea. If you're new to content creation or are only active on one or two platforms, consider creating the five pieces for those platforms. For me, diversifying is key as I'm active on several. Perhaps a blog post, a tutorial video, a short TikTok, a product comparison, and an Instagram post with all the tools and products used.

3. **Lighting, camera angles and tech prep.** I need to make sure all aspects of the videography are set up.

4. **I call myself the "one take king."** I film to edit, which means I do everything in one take. This will come with experience.

5. **Editing.** The one-take filming approach simplifies my editing process once the filming is done.

6. **Uploading.** Uploading and optimizing the video for YouTube.

7. **Schedule in advance.** I schedule the videos to go live at the same time Monday through Friday.

Rinse and Repeat!

Section 2: The WHAT

My WHAT: *Create engaging content that helps people in the hairstyling industry while staying true to who I am instead of chasing trends.*

Your WHAT includes your products, services, and content. It's how you deliver value to your audience.

At the beginning of building my brand, it took a few months to figure out how I would help people. My WHY was crystal clear: to help people be successful in the beauty industry. But what was that going to look like in action? That is where things got real, and I had to determine what I could offer to make that happen.

Let me be very clear: when you don't know exactly WHAT you're offering, the WHY doesn't matter. I have seen people who had an amazing purpose with passion fail because they simply couldn't turn it into something concrete. They had the drive but no direction.

Your WHAT gets tested every single day. It is no longer about the idea; it's about the execution. When I started creating and launching products, each needed to deliver real value. Your WHAT brings your purpose into reality by turning it into action.

Think about it this way: When I started TheSalonGuy®'s YouTube channel, I couldn't just talk about wanting to help hairstylists. I had to create specific tutorials—educational content and products that solve real problems. Your WHAT is where purpose meets practice.

In this section, we will get tactical about your WHAT. No vague ideas, no maybes. We will define precisely what you'll create, who it's for, and how it delivers value.

We'll cover:

- How to identify your true expertise
- Creating offers that people actually want
- Building content that matters
- Making sure everything you do serves your purpose

I already had you create content earlier in the book, and I will ask you to create more in the chapters ahead. It's important to keep refining the content you put out until you feel it consistently hits the mark when it comes to your brand identity and what you have to offer. The first step was simply to get started, which we worked on in the chapters on WHY. The WHAT chapters ahead are designed to help you refine your offer in a way that honors your WHY.

Your WHAT is waiting. Not in some fancy business plan but in your skills, experience, and ability to help others.

Let's make your purpose practical. Take Jimmy Donaldson, better known as MrBeast™. His WHY wasn't just to be famous on YouTube—it was to create the most **engaging, high-impact videos possible** and give back to people in a massive way. Unlike most content creators who chase viral trends, he focused on reinvesting everything into making his content bigger, better, and more meaningful.

His early videos weren't polished, but his WHY kept him going. He started with simple challenge videos, but as his resources grew, his WHAT evolved naturally—high-production, challenge-based content that captivated millions. He went from counting to 100,000 on camera to giving away houses, cars, and even an entire island. His videos weren't just about entertainment; they were about impact.

Because his WHY was rooted in **giving back and making the most engaging content possible**, it paved the way for new opportunities—MrBeast Burger, Feastables, and large-scale philanthropy. His success proves that if your WHY is strong, your WHAT will follow and open up massive opportunities.

Now that you've established your WHY, it's time to figure out your WHAT. Just like MrBeast's purpose of creating high-impact videos led to a global empire, your WHY should influence what you create, sell, or share. Without a solid WHAT, your brand remains just an idea.

Your WHAT is where things get real—it's the bridge between your mission and the tangible products, services, or content you offer to the world. Let's dive in and define exactly how to bring your WHY to life. What is one thing you could create that aligns with your WHY? Write it down before moving forward.

QUICK START GUIDE: THE WHAT ACCELERATOR

Ready to turn your expertise into actual offerings? This guide helps you quickly identify WHAT you'll create, sell, and share with your audience. In the next 30 minutes, you'll map out your expertise, choose your core offerings, and plan next first content pieces.

Think of the Quick Start Guide as your rapid prototyping session. We will build the skeleton of your brand offerings right now. So, grab a timer and something to write with. Let's turn your WHY into a concrete WHAT.

Launch Plan
30-Minute Expertise Mapping

10 Minutes:
- List your top skills
- Write down everything you're good at in your field

10 Minutes:
- Identify problem-solving skills
- What types of problems do you help people solve?

10 Minutes:
- Define your unique value
- What makes your approach different from others?

Your Core Offerings

Choose 2-3 from the following:
- **Digital Products:** Online books, courses, and templates
- **Services:** Coaching, consulting, pre-prepared content

- **Physical Products:** Branded merchandise, tools, and equipment
- **Content:** Premium content, subscriptions, and memberships

Quick Content Strategy

Create your first 5 pieces
- Problem-solving tutorial
- Behind-the-scenes look at your process
- Quick tips or hacks in your field
- Success story or case study
- Education piece about your industry

Keep each piece under 5 minutes or 1000 words

Chapter 5:
WHAT Are Your Brand Offerings?

Now, let's look at WHAT you're going to create. Your brand offerings represent the heart of your business, providing true value to those who need it.

Why Clear Brand Offerings Matter

Look, in today's market, you can't just throw stuff out there and hope it sticks.

Your offerings need to:

- Solve a specific problem
- Be easy to understand
- Deliver undeniable value
- Have a clear target customer
- Create measurable transformation

TheSalonGuy® Story

When I launched TheSalonGuy®, I was laser-focused on my WHY. I wasn't chasing fame or money. I wanted to share my knowledge and experience to help others grow. There were difficult moments when views were low, and sales were slow, but I kept going. That's what allowed me to build successful products, launch HairAdvisor, and create educational content that hairstylists rely on today.

Types of Brand Offerings

Let me show you exactly WHAT you can offer. It's common for people to believe they can only sell one thing. But that's a misconception. Your expertise can take many shapes.

Every great offering starts with focus. Pick one area that matches your skills, make it a success, and then look to expand your reach.

How to Define Your Brand Offerings

Here's how you can approach this in easy, practical steps:

1. **Start with the Problem You Solve**
   - Ask yourself:
     - What struggles does my audience face?
     - How can I fix these problems better than anyone?
     - What solution am I uniquely qualified to provide?

2. **Choose Offerings That Match Your Expertise**
   - Stick to WHAT you know best
   - Make sure it aligns with your WHY
   - Build on your strengths

3. **Be Specific, Not General**
   - Instead of:
     - "Hair Care Products"
   - Say:
     - "Salon-Quality Sea Salt Spray for Effortless Waves"

4. **Define the Value Proposition**
   - Your audience needs to know:
     - Why your offering matters
     - How it will improve their life
     - What makes it different from alternatives

5. **Keep It Simple and Clear**
   - Focus on 2-3 core offerings at first
   - Make sure each one clearly communicates:
     - What exactly you're providing
     - Who it's perfect for
     - What problem it solves

TheSalonGuy® Story

Each offering in my brand was built on my expertise in hair education and styling. I didn't try to be everything to everyone. I focused on what I knew best and built from there. That's why my audience trusts my recommendations.

Let me share a real-world example of how I turned these principles into a seven-figure success story with my hero product, Tidal Wave.

I created Tidal Wave to be a product that would provide results with less effort, fewer product and instant results. I then created videos and tutorials using that product to show my audience the value it brings to my work. This helped me scale up and expand my brand. It became my hero product. The advantage of being a professional stylist for over 30 years is what has helped me launch products that are effective for consumers. My Tidal Wave story demonstrates that success comes from aligning expertise with market opportunities and executing a strategy.

Use this QR code to see how I transformed a regular, everyday product into a seven-figure success story. This breakdown details how knowledge of trends, professional relationships, and focused content created a hero product: Tidal Wave.

You will see exactly how the art of scaling focuses on one item's success so that you can create a blueprint to scale your business.

Take Action: Define Your Offerings

Your offerings bridge what your audience needs and the value you provide.

Begin with something specific, put quality first, and grow from there.

Soon, we'll focus on creating content that builds strong connections. Master these exercises first, and the rest of your brand will thrive. You should already have completed number one below. Now it's time to put your core offerings to use.

1. **List Your Core Offerings (2-3 max)**
   - o What specific problems do they solve?
   - o Who are they perfect for?
   - o How do they provide value?

2. **Write Your Value Propositions**
   - o For each offering, complete:
   - o "This [product/service] helps [specific audience] achieve [specific result] by [your unique method]"

3. **Test Your Ideas**
   - o Share your offerings with potential customers
   - o Get feedback on clarity and value
   - o Refine based on responses

Chapter 6: WHAT Value-Driven Content Should You Create?

By now, we know content is the heartbeat of your brand. It's your way of reaching your audience, demonstrating your knowledge, and establishing credibility.

But let's cut to the chase.

Content is not just posting frequency. It's not about being active on social media just to be seen as active. Everything you put out should have meaning. It has to solve real problems and not just take up space in your audience's timelines.

Why Value-Driven Content Matters

Every day, your audience is scrolling through endless content. Most of it? Pure noise. You're just adding to that noise if your content isn't valued. Without value-driven content:

- Your audience will scroll past
- Your engagement drops
- Your brand becomes forgettable
- Your products won't sell
- Your expertise gets questioned

But when you consistently deliver value? That's when everything changes. Your audience starts looking forward to your posts. They save your content. They share it with friends. They trust your recommendations. And most importantly? They keep coming back for more.

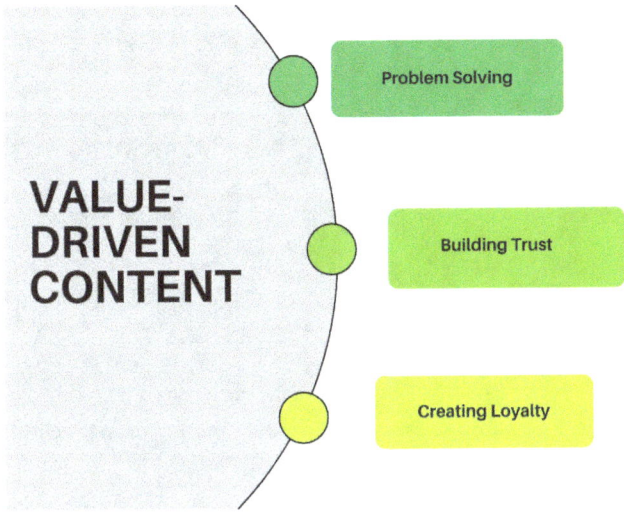

Value isn't optional. It's essential for building a brand that lasts. But WHAT exactly makes content valuable?

What Makes Content Valuable?

For content to be worthy, it must enhance your audience's life or business. It's not about what you want to say; it's about delivering what they need.

Your content must do at least one of the following:

1. Educate – Teach your audience something new or useful.
2. Inspire – Motivate them with stories, experiences, or results.
3. Entertain – Make them laugh or feel emotionally connected.
4. Inform – Provide industry updates, tips, or expert advice.

Here's how to turn these concepts into a straightforward framework for measuring and producing value-added content.

Value vs. Fluff Content

Value Content	VS	Fluff Content
• Solves specific problems • Shows clear expertise • Builds lasting trust • Creates real transformation		• Generic advice • Copies trending topics • Focuses on quick views • No real value included in content

If your content isn't hitting at least one of these marks, it needs work. Now, let's get into the exact steps of creating content that delivers real value.

How to Create Value-Driven Content

Let me explain exactly how to create professional video content without breaking the bank. I started with just my phone, and you can, too.

1. Know Your Audience Inside and Out

You can't produce valuable content without knowing who you are speaking to.

Ask Yourself:
- What is the pain my audience experiences?
- What are the questions they are repeating often?
- What format do they like to see their information: videos, blogs, or social posts?

Example from my business:
- I create YouTube videos for hairstylists because they want practical, easy-to-follow tutorials that they can apply immediately.

2. Solve One Problem Per Piece of Content

Don't try to cure world hunger in one post. Instead, focus on one particular challenge and conquer it. When I create content, each piece has a mission.

Examples from my business:
- "How to Get the Perfect Beach Waves" (Tutorial)
- "Top 5 Hair Products for Fine Hair" (Product Guide)
- "How to Build Your Personal Brand as a Hairstylist" (Educational Video)

Tip: Be direct and get to the point. Don't overcomplicate the message.

3. Share Your Expertise Generously

Give your best advice for free. People will trust you more when they see the real value you bring.

Example from my business:
- When I started sharing detailed styling techniques on YouTube, people thought I was crazy. "Why give it away?" they asked. But that generosity built an empire.

4. Use Clear, Actionable Language

Never use gray or general statements. Allow your audience to be sure of WHAT they will do after going through your content.

Example from my business:
- Instead of: "Here's a tip for better hair."
- Say: "Apply 'Tidal Wave' sea salt spray on damp hair, scrunch lightly, and let it air dry for effortless beach waves."

5. Be Consistent

Success comes in the form of showing up. If you are putting out content daily, weekly, or biweekly, that needs to happen on a scheduled basis.

Example from my business:
- Stick to consistent messaging
- Start videos with a warm, welcoming introduction
- Content is engaging, friendly, funny, and knowledgeable

Tip: Batch create content to avoid last minute stress.

6. Engage and Respond

Content isn't a one-way street. Give responses to comments, answer DMs, or engage with the community. Building loyalty with people and humanizing a brand works here.

Example from my business:
- I've built lasting relationships by responding to YouTube comments, listening to feedback, and adjusting my content accordingly.

TheSalonGuy® Story

When I started my brand, I made a decision that shaped everything: every piece of content had to solve a real problem. My first video wasn't perfect—it was just me and my phone, showing how to do a basic men's haircut. But it solved a specific problem stylists faced. That video led to more requests, more tutorials, and eventually, a community of professionals helping each other grow.

Every single piece of content you create should be designed to move your audience closer to their goals. You're not just creating content; you're building solutions, trust, and relationships. Next, we're going to take this focus on value and turn it into streamlined content creation that works *for* you, not against you, to avoid burnout.

Types of Value-Driven Content You Can Create

Most people overcomplicate this part. They try to do everything, everywhere, all at once. That's a recipe for burnout, not success.

Don't overcomplicate this. Focus on these proven content types that consistently deliver value.

Take a look at the table below to get a good idea of what this means.

You do not have to create every type of content. Choose one or two varieties that play to your strengths and the needs of your audience. Get those right first, and then you can expand. Doing a few great things is always better than doing everything poorly.

Now that you know what types of content work, let's talk about how to make it look professional, even if you're just starting with basic equipment.

Creating Professional Video Content

1. **Get the essential equipment but keep it simple.** Don't get caught up in expensive gear. Start with these basics:
   - Camera: Your smartphone is enough to start. I filmed my first 100 videos on an iPhone
   - Microphone: Clear audio matters more than video quality. A basic Lavalier mic ($20-30) will work
   - Lighting: Natural window light or a basic ring light ($30-50)
   - Tripod: Steady shots are essential. Get a solid phone tripod ($15-20)

2. **Set up your filming space.** Your environment matters, but it doesn't need to be fancy.
   - Choose a clean, uncluttered background
   - Position lighting in front to avoid shadows
   - Find a quiet room (early morning works best)
   - Keep it professional but authentic to your brand

3. **Follow a simple filming process.** Here's my exact filming workflow:
   - *Pre-Production*
     - Write bullet points (not full scripts)
     - Keep intros under 15 seconds
     - Plan your key points
   - *Recording*
     - Test audio/video before full takes
     - Maintain eye contact with camera
     - Speak clearly and naturally
     - Film extra B-roll for transitions
   - *Quality Checks*
     - Review audio levels
     - Check lighting consistency
     - Confirm focus is sharp

- Watch for background distractions

4. **Master basic editing.** Keep it simple but professional.
   - *Software*
     - Start with iMovie (free) or Premiere Rush
     - Focus on basic cuts and transitions
     - Don't overdo effects
   - *Process*
     - Cut out mistakes and pauses
     - Add your branding (logo, colors)
     - Keep transitions clean and simple
     - Export in correct format for each platform

TheSalonGuy® Story

When I started my YouTube channel, I had no video experience whatsoever. My initial setup? My phone propped up with books next to a window. The audio wasn't great, the lighting was basic, but the content helped people. That's what mattered. As the channel grew, I slowly upgraded my gear. But here's what I have learned: better equipment doesn't make better content. Focus on the value first, then on the production quality. Your audience cares more about solving their problems than perfect production.

All this technical stuff might seem overwhelming. But your audience cares more about the value you provide than the camera you use. Let's put all this into action right now.

Take Action: Launch Your First Value Piece

Value comes from solving real problems, not fancy production.

 Start with WHAT you have and focus on helping your audience get results.

Now that you have determined your content strategy, it's almost time to move on to the section where you tackle the barricades holding your WHAT back. But before we do, try this:

Choose Your Topic:
- List 3 problems your audience faces
- Pick the one you can solve best
- Outline your solution in 3-5 steps

Create Your Content:
- Film a tutorial or write a guide
- Focus on clarity over production
- Include specific action steps

Test and Polish:
- Show it to 3 people in your target audience
- Get feedback on clarity and value
- Make quick improvements

Launch and Learn:
- Publish on your main platform
- Share behind-the-scenes of creation
- Track audience response

Chapter 7: Building a Strong WHAT

A person can have a brilliant WHY, be fired up about changing the industry, and have the drive and the vision. But when it comes to actually creating something people can use, buy, or learn from?

 They freeze. This is because their WHAT is weak, unfocused, or nonexistent. I've watched brilliant creators crash and burn because they couldn't translate their WHY into something tangible. They had the vision but not the vehicle.

Your WHAT is that vehicle, and it's time to ensure yours is built to last.

The Myth of "I'm Not an Expert"

Let's discuss one of the major roadblocks I find that prevents people from getting started: what I call the "expert" myth. I don't know how many talented professionals I have watched sit on the sidelines because they are not "qualified enough" to share their knowledge. That's nonsense.

If you can consistently help someone get from point A to point B in your field, you're an expert to them.

That's it. No fancy credentials required.

Expertise = Knowing enough to help others.

If that's not simple enough, I don't know what is.

Think about that for a moment. That's real expertise. It's not about being the best in the world; it's about being the guide someone needs right now.

Reality Check!

Before moving on, take a moment to ask yourself these questions honestly.

1. What do I know that others find valuable?
2. What do others ask me regularly?
3. What experience do I have that others can learn from?

These answers, not years of work experience or the size of your following, reflect your actual level of expertise. Don't obsess over being as good as someone else or as good as an arbitrary benchmark. Take, instead, the expertise you do have today and use it in ways to help others win.

Common Expertise Pitfalls to Avoid

To be clear, here are the four major mistakes I see people making with their expertise.

1. **Trying to Be Everything to Everyone**

   - *As much as we want to, we can't be the best at everything.*
     - **Example:** A marketing expert working with businesses in every industry is trying to spread themselves too thin, and clients are unsure where to focus.
   - *Pick your lane and own it.*
     - **Example:** A personal fitness trainer specializing **in** weight reduction for females over 40 is a good brand when it sticks to its core service instead of trying to solve everybody's problems.
   - *Going niche brings the right crowd into your court.*

- **Example:** An interior designer specializing in ecological design would attract those who believe in saving the environment rather than appealing to everyone's tastes.

2. **Faking Expertise**

- *Nothing kills trust quicker than faking it.*
  - **Example:** An entrepreneur pretending to know everything about a topic loses trust because **they** can't answer tough questions honestly.
- *Be honest about WHAT you know and don't know.*
  - **Example:** A tech expert admits they don't know about one specific topic but suggests where to find more information, showing honesty instead of pretending to know everything.
- *Your audience respects authenticity over perfection.*
  - **Example:** A writer shares their struggles with a project, and their audience **connects** more because they appreciate the realness instead of a perfect story.

3. **Not Updating Your Skills**

- *Your industry is changing, and so should you.*
  - **Example:** A graphic designer who stays updated **with** new tools and trends offers better services than one who sticks to old methods.
- *Set aside time each week to learn.*
  - **Example:** A personal trainer invests one hour **weekly** in learning new exercises and techniques to be one step ahead of others who have not kept up with their learning.
- *Follow industry leaders and stay current.*

- **Example:** A marketer follows various top experts, **reads** blogs to stay updated about new strategies, and does not depend on methods no longer bringing in results.

4. **Shutting Yourself Off to Feedback**

- *Your audience tells you WHAT they need.*
  - **Example:** A fashion blogger finds that their followers are requesting budget-friendly outfit ideas and begins to post those, giving **their** audience what they desire.
- *Pay attention to common questions.*
  - **Example:** A career coach receives the same questions **repeatedly**. She creates a list of answers on her website so others can benefit.
- *Let feedback shape your content.*
  - **Example:** A video game streamer listens to **feedback**, asks for more tips and creates a tutorial series to meet the needs of their viewers.

These pitfalls are real reasons so many talented professionals never reach their full potential. By staying aware of these common mistakes, you can focus on what matters: delivering genuine value to your audience.

The other important part of building a strong WHAT is to avoid being too generic in your brand offerings.

Common Brand Offering Mistakes to Avoid

This is what I learned the hard way so that you won't have to.

- **Trying to Offer Too Much**
  - *Quality beats quantity every time.*

- Example: A restaurant with too many items on its menu loses the focus on the dishes it does best, so customers do not know WHAT to order.
  - *Master one offering before adding another.*
    - Example: A clothing brand first masters the art of making the comfiest T-shirts, then produces jackets to ensure the best main product.
  - *Don't spread yourself too thin.*
    - Example: A startup trying to sell several services simultaneously will not do any of them well, frustrating customers and wasting resources.

- **Lack of Clarity**
  - *If people don't understand it, they won't buy it.*
    - Example: No matter how good a tech product is, it will turn off customers due to confusing instructions and unclear benefits.
  - *Every offering should solve a clear problem.*
    - Example: A fitness app with too many features might turn off clients looking for a simple step-tracking app.
  - *Make your value proposition crystal clear.*
    - Example: A small business clearly explains on its website what it offers and how the product benefits customers, making it easy for anyone to understand why they should purchase.

- **Ignoring Customer Needs**
  - *Build what they need, not what you think they want.*
    - Example: The telephone company that continually adds bells and whistles instead of improving its battery life is off-target.
  - *Listen to feedback and adapt.*

- Example: An online store notices that customers want quicker delivery and it adjusts its shipping process to meet the demand.
    - ○ *Solve real problems, not imaginary ones.*
        - Example: A new app that solves a problem users do not have will fail, even if it is impressive in terms of technology, because it does not fill an actual need.

- **No Unique Selling Point (USP)**
    - ○ *Stand out or get lost in the crowd.*
        - Example: A bakery focusing on vegan and gluten-free treats stands out from the competition, while others offering the same old baked goods blend in.
    - ○ *Define WHAT makes you different.*
        - Example: A personal trainer who offers flexible online coaching for busy professionals clearly states that their program is tailored for people with hectic schedules.
    - ○ *Communicate your value proposition.*
        - Example: A hotel advertises that it is pet-friendly and has environmentally friendly amenities, clearly stating why it is the best choice for green-minded pet owners.

TheSalonGuy® Story

When I developed my first products, I started with the essentials. Based on my experience as a stylist, I wanted to solve problems for my audience. That focus allowed me to create a small range of products that I knew would work. I wasn't trying to be everything to everybody. I knew my area of expertise, haircutting and styling, and I stayed in my lane! That clarity helped me gain trust with my audience and establish real authority in my niche.

Every single mistake I have mentioned has come from a real-life experience that took place around me in each particular field. What you offer doesn't have to be perfect, but it should be planned and intentional. Continue to intentionally work on developing what genuinely serves your target audience's interests by means of upholding your actual experience.

Building a Strong WHAT
Evaluate your current position • List your top 3 skills • List 3 areas where you lack expertise • List what you currently offer • Find the gaps between what you know, what you offer, and what you still need to learn
Focus on your expertise • Choose one of the 3 skills above to focus on first • Create content that shows what you know • Build trust by creating content that offers consistent value
Refine your offerings • Ensure each offering solves a real problem • Highlight the value in your offerings • Improve your business by learning from feedback

This framework already breaks down the essential elements of a strong WHAT into clear, actionable components. Each piece builds on the next to form a sturdy structure for your expertise and offerings. By paying attention to these basic elements and avoiding common pitfalls, you are building something that will make a difference.

Take Action: Strengthen Your WHAT

 Your WHAT needs to be strong enough to deliver on your WHY.

No more hiding behind the "I'm not an expert" excuse.

Your audience needs WHAT you know. Start sharing it today.

As we explore your business's HOW, remember that your WHAT needs to be rock-solid. First, complete these exercises to ensure your foundation is solid. Begin with something specific, prioritize quality, and grow from there.

1. **Expertise Audit**
   o Write down your top 3 skills
   o List the problems you can solve
   o Identify your unique approach

2. **Offering Analysis**
   o Review each of your current offerings
   o Rate their clarity and value (1-10)
   o List specific improvements needed

3. **Action Plan**
   o Choose one expertise to focus on
   o Plan your next 30 days of content
   o Set specific goals for improvement

Zero to Launch:
Get Your WHAT Going

Now that you've defined your strengths and offerings, it's time to put them into action. This plan simplifies the launch process, turning what might seem overwhelming into a series of clear, achievable steps. Whether you're launching a digital product, service, or content, this guide will take you from concept to execution.

Action Plan: Launching Your WHAT
3-Day Launch Plan

Day 1: Research & Planning
- Research 3 competitors in your field
- Survey 5 potential clients about their needs

Day 2: Creation & Testing
- Create a minimally viable version for your core offer
- Test with 2-3 trusted contacts

Day 3: Preparation & Setup
- Set up sales page and description
- Set up payment and delivery system

30-Day Content Calendar

Weeks 1-2: Educational Content (6 pieces)
- How-to
- Tutorials
- Expert Tips

Week 3: Building Authority (3 pieces)
- Case Studies
- Insider Insights

• Success Stories

Week 4: Engagement (3 pieces)
- Behind the scenes
- Q&As
- Community Features

<table>
<tr><td style="background-color:green;color:white;text-align:center">Launch Success List</td></tr>
<tr><td>

- Launch content created
- Test with trusted members of the target audience
- Early feedback incorporated
- Sales page & description complete
- Payment system tested
- Support system in place

</td></tr>
</table>

Section 3: The HOW

My HOW: *My tactical approach to filming, editing, posting, engaging, and scaling my brand.*

Your WHY drives you. Your WHAT defines you. But your HOW makes you unstoppable.

I've seen countless people with amazing purpose and brilliant ideas fail because they couldn't execute. They had the vision but stumbled on implementation. That's why this section is crucial.

It might sound corny, but it really is where dreams become reality.

When I started TheSalonGuy®, I didn't just have a mission to help hair stylists succeed (my WHY) or a plan to create educational content (my WHAT). I needed a concrete filming, editing, posting, engaging, and scaling system. That tactical approach (the HOW) turned a vision into a seven-figure brand.

Your HOW is your battle plan. It's about action and results. In these next chapters, we'll break down exactly how to take action with clear focus, ensuring each move is intentional and effective. We'll then look at how to grow your business without burning out, finding a pace that allows for steady progress while keeping your energy up. We'll also cover how to stand out in a crowded market, ensuring your brand captures attention and stays relevant. You'll learn how to become the face of your brand, building a genuine connection with your audience. Finally, we'll learn about building systems that last so you can keep things running smoothly and sustainably. Each step will help you create a solid, lasting foundation for success.

We'll cover:

- Step-by-step execution strategies
- Proven scaling tactics
- Content creation systems
- Personal branding frameworks
- Time-tested productivity methods

No fluff, no maybes, no "wouldn't it be nice." Just tactical steps you can implement today.

Your HOW is waiting. Not in some fancy business strategy or complex theory but in practical, actionable steps. These next chapters will give you the exact blueprint to turn your purpose and plans into reality.

Let's make it happen.

QUICK START GUIDE:
THE HOW ACCELERATOR

This is where action meets strategy. You know your WHY. You've defined your WHAT. Now, it's time to execute. This guide gives you a concrete framework to start implementing everything we've built so far. The next 48 hours are critical. Instead of getting lost in endless planning, we'll set up systems, create content, and build momentum. Keep this guide handy; it's your tactical playbook for turning plans into reality.

Quick Start Guide: Executing Your HOW
48-Hour Execution Framework
Morning of Day 1: System Setup • Content calendar • Task management • File organization
Afternoon Day 1: Content Creation • Templates • Outlines • Batch content plan
Morning Day 2: First Batch • Produce the first week's content in one focused session, continuing into the afternoon if necessary
Scaling Checklist
Automate: • Social media scheduling • Email sequences • Customer onboarding

Delegate:
- Content editing
- Customer support
- Administrative tasks

Staying Relevant

Weekly Actions
- Engage with audience comments (30 minutes daily)
- Monitor industry trends (1 hour weekly)
- Review analytics and adjust (1 hour weekly)
- Network with industry peers (1 hour weekly)
- Update 1 piece of content (2 hours weekly)

Schedule these tasks. What gets scheduled gets done.

You now have the basic framework to execute your brand strategy. The 48-hour plan gets you started, the scaling checklist keeps you growing, and the relevancy strategy ensures you stay valuable to your audience.

Don't try to implement everything at once. Start with the 48-hour framework, then gradually incorporate the scaling and relevancy elements as you build momentum. The detailed chapters will give you deeper insights, but this framework ensures you're taking action now.

Execution beats perfection. Start today.

Chapter 8: HOW to Execute

Ideas are worthless without execution.

You can dream up the best brand concept or content strategy in the world, but if you can't execute it, it will be another idea collecting dust.

I have seen dozens of super-talented creators fail not because their ideas were not worth much but because they could never transform them into tangible output.

Why Execution Matters More Than Ideas

Here's the brutal truth: Success is not about having the right plan; it's about showing up, being consistent, and executing when you don't feel like it.

Let's unpack what real execution actually looks and feels like. It's not just about working hard. It is where three critical components merge:

EXECUTION

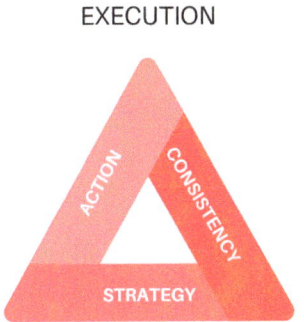

Consistency keeps you moving forward! Strategy ensures you are going in the right direction.

Action turns plans into results. Miss any one of these elements, and your execution falls apart.

Knowing execution is one thing; implementation is quite another. You can know everything in the world about what makes execution tick, and yet, without a clear roadmap to follow, you'll still struggle to make progress.

That means we've got to break this down into something practical: a step-by-step execution blueprint you can start using today. No theory, just tactical steps that get results.

Allow me to take you behind the scenes and show you precisely how I execute my content creation process in my studio.

Get an exclusive look inside my production studio and learn my complete content creation workflow, from one-take filming techniques to editing software choices, as I consistently reveal how I create and publish content.

Whether working with a professional studio or just getting started with a smartphone, you will come away with practical strategies for efficient content creation that get results.

As I showed in the video, great execution doesn't depend on high-end tools. It hinges on building systems that fit your needs and maintaining steady effort. Let's map out how to create an execution strategy that works for you.

How to Build an Execution Blueprint

Your execution blueprint is a simple, tactical battle plan. This is your step-by-step guide for turning ideas into action.

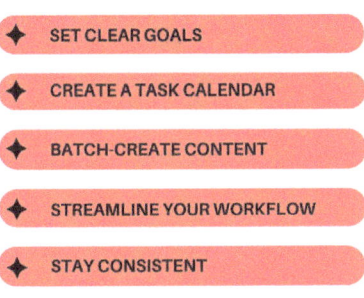

EXECUTION BLUEPRINT

- ✦ SET CLEAR GOALS
- ✦ CREATE A TASK CALENDAR
- ✦ BATCH-CREATE CONTENT
- ✦ STREAMLINE YOUR WORKFLOW
- ✦ STAY CONSISTENT
- ✦ TRACK, REVIEW, ADJUST

1. Set Clear Goals

You wouldn't go on a road trip without knowing your destination, right? The same goes for your brand. You need a clear, measurable goal to guide and keep you on track.

What To Track:
- Content Goals (Example: Post 2 YouTube videos weekly)
- Revenue Targets (Example: Hit $10K monthly from products)
- Growth Metrics (Example: Gain 5,000 email subscribers in 90 days)

Tip: Write down 3 to 5 specific goals for the next 3 to 6 months. Ensure that those goals are visible, timebound, and result-oriented.

2. Create Your Task Calendar

That's where many go wrong: trying to just "wing it" and wonder why they are always falling behind. Your calendar is your battle plan—stick to it like your brand's life depends on it because it does.

Essential Calendar Components:
- Content Topics & Publishing Dates
- Production Deadlines (Filming, Editing, Review)
- Marketing Tasks (Social Posts, Email Campaigns)

Daily Tasks:
- Engage with Audience
- Respond to Comments/DMs

Weekly Tasks:
- Film Content
- Edit Videos
- Review Analytics

Monthly Tasks:
- Launch New Products
- Host Live Events
- Review Performance

3. Batch-Create Content

Here's a secret that changed everything for me: batch creation. Instead of scrambling to make content daily, block out focused time to create multiple pieces at once.

Example Batch Schedule:
- Monday: Script 3 videos
- Tuesday: Film all 3 videos
- Wednesday: Edit videos and create thumbnails

4. Streamline Your Workflow

Efficiency isn't just about working hard—it's about working smart. Create systems that automate execution.

Key Systems to Build:
- Pre-filming checklist
- Content templates

- Automated scheduling
- Quality control process

5. Stay Consistent

Let me be clear: consistency beats perfection every time. I'd rather see you post good content regularly than perfect content occasionally.

Consistency Rules:
- Follow your calendar religiously
- Create content in advance
- Stay flexible but never quit
- Show up even when motivation is low

6. Track, Review, Adjust

Your execution plan isn't set in stone. Track what works, ditch what doesn't, and keep improving.

Monthly Review Checklist:
- Best performing content?
- Time-consuming tasks?
- Areas for improvement?
- Audience feedback?

This blueprint is the exact framework I've used to build multiple successful brands. Each component works together to create a machine that turns ideas into reality.

TheSalonGuy® Story

When I started my brand, I knew execution would be all-or-nothing. I created a military-style production schedule and stuck to it like my life depended on it. Every Sunday night, I mapped out my week: Mondays for filming, Tuesdays for editing, and Wednesdays for scheduling. Rain or shine, tired or energized, I showed up—no excuses.

The hardest part is doing it. Choose the most difficult, annoying task you want to do the least and do that first. You will feel a huge sense of accomplishment, and it will build a tolerance you can't avoid.

Take Action: Execute Your Blueprint

The hardest part is just to start.

Not when the time is right—that day never comes. Take this blueprint, adapt it to your schedule, and start executing today.

Your brand is waiting.

Chapter 9: HOW to Scale

Scaling your brand means going BIGGER than the current version.

You know: "More products! More content! More revenue!"

But... scaling isn't about working until your eyes bleed.

I learned that lesson the hard way, pulling 18-hour days until I nearly crashed and burned. Most creators try to scale by throwing more hours at the problem.

 It's like trying to put out a fire with gasoline... you'll just end up burnt.

Rather, you have to do the right things, better and faster.

HOW? Build the right systems BEFORE you scale.

Real Scaling vs. Fake Scaling

Scale without strategy is organized chaos. I have watched brilliant creators implode because they confused movement for progress. They post more content, launch more products, and burn through more cash... but their brand isn't actually growing; it's just bloated.

Real vs. Fake Scaling

Real Scaling	Fake Scaling
• Systems run the show	• You do it all and run yourself ragged
• Quality rises with quantity	• Quality drops with quantity
• Strategic team growth	• Hiring out of desperation
• More revenue than expenses	• Expenses eat profits
• Brand stregnthens	• Brand gets diluted

VS

Knowing the difference between real and fake scaling practices is how you will build something that lasts without burning out. Let me share some hard-earned wisdom on how to prevent this when scaling your brand.

Use this QR code to watch as I reveal why most creators give up too soon and how to avoid this common pitfall.

Learn how to identify what's working in your content, understand the importance of authentic credentials, and discover how to scale sustainably without burning out. This video will give you important insights on sustaining momentum when growth gets hard.

Your Power Zone is where your unique talents create maximum impact with minimum drain. Building systems around it is where the real scaling takes place.

Finding Your Power Zone,
Turning It Into Product

A lesson learned while building TheSalonGuy® is that you can't be good at everything, but you have to be great at something. You have zeroed in on what I call your "Power Zone," that sweet spot where your unique talents create maximum impact.

POWER ZONE

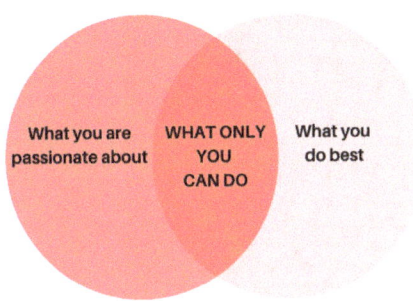

Here are examples of what it can look like when creators find their Power Zone:

1. A musician realizes his Power Zone isn't only in performing but in helping others express their emotions through songwriting. He now runs an online academy for aspiring musicians.
2. A teacher recognizes that her strength lies not only in the classroom but also in helping parents support their children's learning at home. So, she developed a popular guide for homeschooling families.
3. A writer finds that her gift is not just writing but helping other people find their voices. She runs a very successful new-author workshop series.

Once you've identified your Power Zone, it's time to convert it into scalable offerings that create passive income.

To do that, consider these Power Questions:

1. What work makes time disappear?
2. Which tasks would you do for free?

3. What do people constantly ask you to teach them?
4. Where do you get the biggest results with the least effort?

Once you've identified your Power Zone, you need to transform it into offerings that generate revenue while staying true to your strengths.

TheSalonGuy® Story

For me, the Power Zone is crystal clear: creating high-impact educational content, developing game-changing products, and developing brand strategy.

Notice what's not in there?

Editing videos or managing social media may be important tasks, but they are not where I create the most value.

The following image will help you turn your Power Zone into profitable product.

HOW TO SCALE: HIGH IMPACT, LOW MAINTENANCE

Digital Products

- Online Courses: Create once, profit forever
- E-books: Automatic delivery and ongoing availability
- Templates: Instant downloads

Memberships

- Premium Content: Exclusive access
- Community Platforms: Recurring revenue

Physical Products

- Automated fulfilment: Hands-off processing
- Drop shipping: No inventory required

Every hour spent outside your Power Zone is an hour stolen from your true impact. Build systems, delegate the rest, and focus on what only you can do.

Finding it is just the first step. The real challenge is scaling up without burning out. Most creators hit a wall because they try to grow by working longer hours. Don't do it; you'll eventually break down.

Instead, let me show you how to build a system that grows while you sleep.

How to Scale Smartly Without Burning Out

When I scaled my workplace from my bathroom studio to a seven-figure operation, I didn't do it by working harder. I did it by working smarter.

Here's the exact framework I used to scale TheSalonGuy® from a solo operation to a seven-figure brand.

Step 1: Build Systems and Automate

Think of your brand like an engine. Right now, you're probably the engine, transmission, and wheels all at once. That's exhausting, and it won't last. Here's how to build a machine that runs without burning you out:

Core Systems

System 1: Content Factory
- Your filming setup
- Editing flow
- Posting sequence
- Quality checks

Step-by-Step Processes:
- Script

- Film
- Edit
- Post with a repeatable workflow

What to Automate:
- Use tools like Buffer, Later, or Hootsuite

System 2: Product Pipeline System
- Testing protocol
- Launch sequence
- Feedback loop
- Improvement cycle

Step-by-Step Processes:
- Research market demand
- Create product prototype
- Test with focus group
- Refine based on feedback
- Set up sales funnel
- Launch and monitor metrics

What to Automate:
- Use Shopify or another eCommerce platform for automatic order processing

System 3: Customer Care System
- Response system
- Problem-solving tree
- Follow-up protocol
- Loyalty builders

Step-by-Step Processes:
- Document common issues
- Create response templates
- Set up ticketing system
- Train support team
- Monitor satisfaction scores

- Review and optimize weekly

What to Automate:
- Use chatbots or hire virtual assistants

When your business runs on systems instead of pure hustle, you can scale without sacrificing your sanity. But systems alone aren't enough. You need the right people to operate and optimize them.

TheSalonGuy® Story

I used Shopify Automation for online orders and shipping notifications when I launched my hair product line, which freed me up to market and create content.

Step 2: Build a Success Team and Delegate

I did try to become a one-man show with TheSalonGuy®, and, boy, that almost broke my back.

Why?

Because behind each "self-made" success story lies an army of supporters ensuring it happens. Your support network is like a power grid. Here's exactly what you need:

Your Mentors
- Industry veterans who've been in the trenches
- Mentors who'll tell you the hard truth
- Advisors who've scaled before you

Your Peers
- Fellow creators who get your struggles
- Industry peers for strategy sharing
- Accountability partners who push you forward

Your Team Members
- Editors who make your content shine
- Support engines that handle customer care
- Social media experts who keep engagement high

These are all the types of people that you need on your success team. But, don't you dare hire an army overnight!

Follow this sequence to find out HOW to pick the right team:

Start with Freelancers
- Test different editors on single videos
- Try virtual assistants for 5-10 hours/week
- Use project-based contractors for specific needs

Graduate to Part-Time Pros
- Convert best freelancers to regular hours
- Establish clear performance metrics
- Create training systems

Scale to Full-Time Forces
- Hire dedicated team members
- Build department structures
- Create career paths

Each connection adds strength; when one part fails, the others keep your lights on. That is why delegating tasks is important to balance responsibilities between yourself, your team, and each member. But before you start delegating, you need to know what to hand off first.

TheSalonGuy® Story

When I first started, I edited every video myself, which took hours. Hiring my first editor felt like a risk, but it freed up a lot of time, allowing me to focus on content creation and product development. That one move helped double my output and revenue within 90 days.

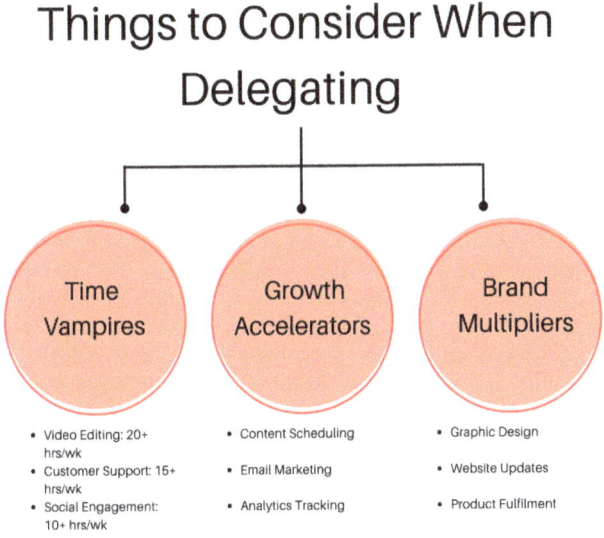

When considering which tasks to delegate, it's important to consider whether the task is high or low maintenance and whether the result is high or low impact.

- Some tasks require constant attention (high maintenance)
- Others thrive with minimal care (low maintenance)
- Some tasks lead to huge results (high impact)
- Others just take up time (low impact)

Your goal?

Focus on the *high-impact, low-maintenance* activities that give you the biggest harvest for the least effort.

Step 3: Build a Time Management Plan

Scaling only works if you have the energy and mental clarity to make smart decisions. To protect your time and avoid burnout, set boundaries.

Work Hours: Set specific working hours and stick to them

Personal Time: Block out time for rest, exercise, and hobbies

Mental Space: Say no to opportunities that don't align with your goals

Once you know what matters most, you have to preserve it.

How?

Stop treating every hour like it's worth the same. *It's not.* Block out the most important items first, then schedule them when you have the most energy to do them well.

Consider the idea of peak, medium, and low energy hours when scheduling tasks and activities. This can help you get more done in less time while performing the most important tasks when you have the most energy. Here's what that might look like.

Match your energy to your tasks for maximum productivity.

Peak Energy Hours (Morning/Early Day):
- Content Creation: Film videos, write scripts, develop new products
- Strategic Planning: Map out launches, review analytics, set goals
- Creative Work: Brainstorm new ideas, solve complex problems

- Important Meetings: Mentor calls, team strategy sessions

Medium Energy Hours (Afternoon):
- Email Management: Respond to important messages
- Content Editing: Review and refine existing work
- Team Management: Check-ins and project updates
- Social Media Engagement: Reply to comments, engage with audience

Low Energy Hours (Evening/End of Day):
- Simple Tasks: Schedule posts, organize files
- Administrative Work: Update calendars, basic documentation
- Light Planning: Review tomorrow's schedule
- Research: Browse industry news, watch competitor content

Time management is about maximizing the impact of the hours you have.

TheSalonGuy® Story

When I started, I worked around the clock. BIG mistake. Now, I film all my content in the morning when I am most productive, do business operations in the afternoon, and save lighter tasks and family time for the evening. This has doubled my productivity while cutting my work hours in half.

So, how do you scale your brand? By working smarter.

When you understand your Power Zone, build strong systems, assemble the right team, and manage your energy effectively, you can grow your brand without burning out.

Take Action: Scale Up!

Knowledge without action is useless. Find your Power Zone, build scalable products, and multiply your impact. Your brand's next level is waiting. Next, I'll teach you how to stay relevant in a rapidly changing market. First, here's your tactical plan to start scaling in the next 48 hours.

Hours 1-2: Power Zone Audit
- List your daily tasks
- Rate energy levels for each
- Identify top 3 revenue generators

Hours 3-4: System Check
- Document core processes
- Spot automation opportunities
- List delegation candidates

By Hour 24: Support Squad Assembly
- Reach out to potential mentors
- Join 2 industry groups
- Post first contractor job

By Hour 48: Scalable Product Planning
- Choose your first offering
- Map out creation timeline
- Set up delivery system

Chapter 10: HOW to Stay Relevant

Relevance isn't optional in today's market.

Your success today is not going to promise your survival tomorrow.

When I started TheSalonGuy®, the beauty industry was completely different. No TikTok, no Reels, no online courses. I have watched some incredible brands fade into obscurity because they couldn't keep up with change.

 From that, I learned something important about staying relevant...

It's not about chasing trends.

It's all about continuously delivering value while growing with your audience.

Why Staying Relevant Is Essential

Competition is everywhere.

New creators are coming into the market, new platforms are emerging, and audience expectations are changing daily. No matter how successful your brand gets, the market keeps on changing.

To survive and thrive, you must adapt, innovate, and stay hooked to your audience. It's about being valuable and indispensable. It's about moving without losing your core.

Staying Relevant

Consistent Innovation 01

Customer Connection 02

Industry Awareness 03

How to Stay Relevant in a Crowded Market

Being relevant is going to be, without question, your number one competitive advantage in today's world.

Lead the change by adapting to it.

HOW? Let's explore proven strategies to help your brand not just survive but thrive in an increasingly competitive landscape.

Step 1: Stay Connected to Your Audience

Keep a close relationship with your audience. It tells you exactly what they need if you're willing to listen.

Engage Daily
- Respond to comments within 24 hours
- Reply to DMs personally
- Read and respond to reviews
- Go live weekly

Run Regular Surveys
- Use Instagram polls for quick feedback
- Send quarterly email surveys
- Create interactive YouTube polls
- Host focus groups for product testing

Listen Actively
- Monitor comment sections for recurring questions
- Track frequently requested topics
- Notice patterns in complaints or praise
- Pay attention to HOW they use your products

The audience fuels success through loyalty and feedback, but relevance comes from sensitivity to industry changes. Here's how to balance them.

TheSalonGuy® Story

When my audience wanted more styling tutorials, I didn't just film more videos; I created a series. Views doubled, and subscribers jumped 40% in three months. Why? Because I gave them exactly what they were asking for.

Step 2: Monitor Industry Trends

Being trendy isn't the goal, but being ahead of the curve is. You must spot trends before they peak and adapt them to your brand's unique voice.

How do you spot trends? This table provides some ideas.

Platform	What to Watch	Frequency
Social Media	Hashtags, Influencer Content	Daily
Competitor Channels	Content Format, Engagement Strategies	Weekly
Industry Reports	Market Data, Consumer Behavior	Monthly
Trade Shows	New Products, Techniques, Strategies	Quarterly

Important: Don't chase every trend!

Ask yourself:
- Does this align with my brand's mission?
- Will this provide real value to my audience?
- Can I add something unique to this trend?

While monitoring the trend keeps you "in the know," what you do with the information matters. That's why strategically refreshing your brand is important to keeping it relevant. Let's see how you can evolve without losing your essence.

Step 3: Refresh Your Brand Consistently

A stagnant brand is a dying brand.

Evolution, not revolution!

You want to stay fresh while maintaining your core identity.

Content Updates
- Launch new content series
- Experiment with emerging platforms
- Update older content with new insights
- Create multi-platform content packages

Visual Branding
- Refresh website design annually
- Update product packaging
- Modernize logo and graphics
- Maintain brand consistency

Product Innovation
- Launch new products quarterly
- Update existing products based on feedback
- Create limited editions
- Test new formats

TheSalonGuy® Story

I decided to expand my product line based on clients' needs to have better-looking hair. Styling products are essential, and I had to expand my range into styling tools, shampoos, conditioners, and digital products.

Step 4: Deliver Exceptional Value

Being good isn't good enough anymore. You must be exceptional at every touchpoint.

Here are some value delivery frameworks. It's all pretty simple when you think about it.

Core Offerings
- Exceed quality expectations
- Provide unexpected extras
- Maintain consistent excellence
- Update based on feedback

Customer Experience
- Personal touch in communications
- Rapid response to issues
- Clear, helpful information
- Above-and-beyond service

Additional Value
- Free educational content
- Exclusive community access
- Behind-the-scenes insights
- Early access to launches

The core of brand loyalty is delivering value. To really amplify your impact, though, you have to expand beyond your own reach, and that's where strategic partnerships come in. Strategic partnerships multiply your reach and credibility.

Remember: choose partners that bring value to your brand, not just any old influencer.

How does collaboration help?

Step 5: Collaborate and Partner

- Exposes your brand to fresh perspectives and new audiences.
- Taps into different market segments, helps learn from others' expertise, and stays connected to emerging trends.
- Shows your audience that you're actively growing and evolving within your industry.

Partnerships expand your audience, but their feedback whets your strategy. Here's how to transform that feedback into impactful changes.

Step 6: Embrace Feedback and Adapt

Every complaint is an opportunity to improve. Every suggestion is potential innovation.

How do you collect feedback?

- Customer surveys
- Social media polls
- Direct messages
- Product reviews
- Analytics data

With this strategy, your marketing boosts visibility and delivers lasting value. Creating a continuous feedback loop turns customer insights into actionable improvements. Having great products and services isn't enough; you must convey your value to the market. That brings us to the next step: master strategic marketing.

STAYING RELEVANT

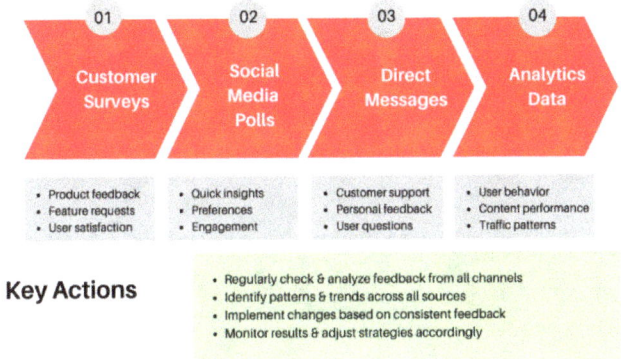

Key Actions
- Regularly check & analyze feedback from all channels
- Identify patterns & trends across all sources
- Implement changes based on consistent feedback
- Monitor results & adjust strategies accordingly

Step 7: Master Strategic Marketing

Marketing is how you stay visible and valuable in your audience's mind. It's much more than mere promotion.

How do you market effectively?

- Content Marketing: Create educational, inspirational, and promotional content
- Social Media Strategy: Post consistently across platforms (2-3 times per week)
- Email Marketing: Build lists and automated sequences
- Launch Strategy: Use multi-platform campaigns for product launches
- Collaboration: Partner with influencers and complementary brands

Take these tips to heart. Even more, memorize these execution tips. After all, it's all about doing.

Marketing Execution Tips

Create lead magnets
Build your email list with valuable downloadable content

Follow the 80/20 rule
80% value content, 20% promotional content

Track analysis
Monitor and optimize performance metrics

Engage daily
Respond to comments and messages consistently

3-Phase launch strategy
Tease, launch, follow-up

Strategic marketing keeps successful brands ahead and others buried in the dust. Consistently applying these tactics will ensure you maintain a strong foothold in your industry and maintain lasting connections with your audience. Relevance is never a fixed point. This framework will keep you ahead of that moving target. If you are consistent, your brand will truly thrive.

Take Action: Stay Relevant, For Crying Out Loud!

Your relevance is earned daily through consistent action and innovation.

Don't even think it's going to happen automatically for one second.

Start with these steps, measure what works, and keep evolving.

48-Hour Relevance Sprint:

- *Day 1:*
    - Audit your content performance
    - Survey your audience

- Review competitor strategies
- List potential innovations

- ***Day 2:***
  - Create content calendar
  - Plan one brand refresh element
  - Reach out to potential partners
  - Set up feedback systems

90-Day Relevance Goals:
- Launch new content series
- Implement one major brand refresh
- Secure two strategic partnerships
- Create one innovative offering

Chapter 11: HOW To Be the Face of Your Brand

These days, people don't just buy products.

They buy into *people*.

You have to put yourself out there.

Front and center.

You have to become the face that everyone associates with what you create.

Maybe it sounds scary, the idea of always having to be "perfect and polished." But it's not scary if you think about it. Not really.

Other than that, all you need to do is just show up consistently as yourself.

You'll learn exactly how to take center stage authentically in this chapter. But first, let's make one thing real: why should putting your face on your brand be such a big deal in today's business landscape?

Why Being the Face of Your Brand Matters

You're not just selling products or services when you put yourself out there.

You are sharing your WHAT.

You are sharing your WHY.

You're sharing your expertise, your journey, and your vision. This matters for several reasons:

WHY BEING THE FACE OF YOUR BRAND MATTERS

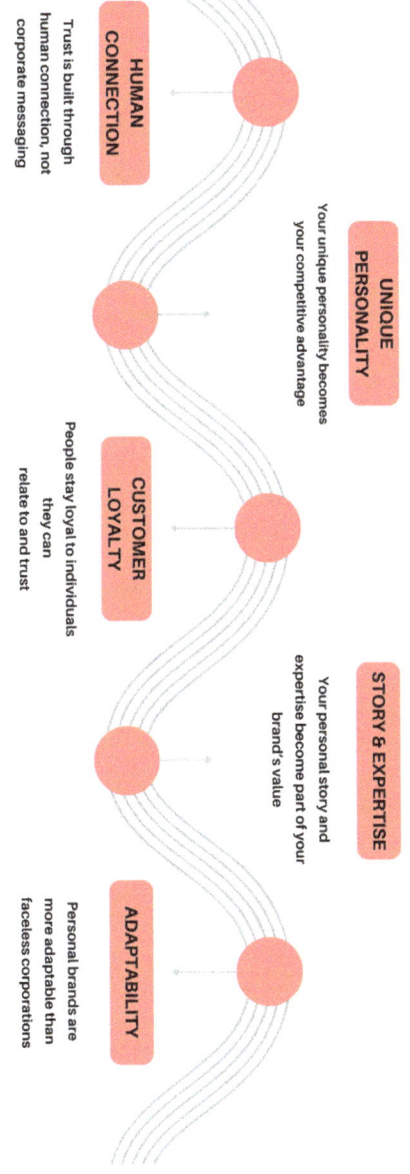

HUMAN CONNECTION

Trust is built through human connection, not corporate messaging

UNIQUE PERSONALITY

Your unique personality becomes your competitive advantage

CUSTOMER LOYALTY

People stay loyal to individuals they can relate to and trust

STORY & EXPERTISE

Your personal story and expertise become part of your brand's value

ADAPTABILITY

Personal brands are more adaptable than faceless corporations

People are bombarded by faceless companies through the media. They want to see that behind them is a real person who has gone through or understands their struggles and who really wishes to help. I've seen countless creators build their personal brands, and the ones who succeed aren't the most talented. They're the most genuine.

By being genuine, you will be seen as a strong face of your brand. When you become the face of your brand, you connect with your audience in a meaningful way. Connecting with your audience transforms followers into long-term supporters.

Personal Brand = Authenticity + Expertise + Consistency + Connection

Use this QR code to see how I turned the curse of being a bald guy talking about hair into a multi-million-viewer success story.

Learn why you have to be the face of your brand, how to be yourself out in front, and why professional polish is way more important than perfection.

In this masterclass, I'll explain the essential elements of a personal brand, one that creates a real connection with your audience.

The power of being the face of your brand is clear, but knowing why it matters isn't enough. You need tactical measures to promote yourself effectively. Let's break down exactly how to do that.

Tactical Steps for Putting Yourself Out There

Now that you understand why being visible matters. Let's break down exactly how to do it.

Each step is designed to help you show up authentically and consistently, even if you're just starting.

Step 1: Think About Your Signature Style (Your WHY and WHAT)

Quit blending in with the crowd. Your individuality is what sets you apart.

This goes back to your WHY.

Your signature style should reflect your core purpose.

This goes back to your WHAT.

Your offerings should shine through in your style.

For example:
- Your style might be more detailed and educational if you teach complex skills.
- If you're inspiring others, your style might be more energetic and motivational.

We're talking about style here in the HOW stage because this is where everything comes together.

Your WHY gives you purpose, your WHAT defines your expertise...

But your HOW...

Especially your personal style...

That is what makes you memorable.

Now that you understand how your style connects to your WHY and WHAT, let's go step-by-step into how this relates to putting yourself out there.

Personal Brand Elements:
- Choose your core topics (stick to 2-3 main themes)
- Develop your speaking style (formal, casual, educational)
- Pick your visual elements (colors, backgrounds, fonts)
- Design your content format (tutorials, vlogs, tips)

Style Guidelines:
- Dress consistently with your brand
- Use the same intro/outro in videos
- Maintain consistent filming locations
- Keep your message aligned with your expertise

Filming Tips for Personal Branding:
- Whenever possible, film in natural light
- Use a clean, simple background
- Always check the audio before recording fully
- Keep your eyes on the camera
- Speak to the camera as if speaking to one person

TheSalonGuy® Story

For me, being TheSalonGuy® isn't just about hair. It's about educating and inspiring others in the industry. My direct, no-nonsense teaching style came from my WHY: Helping others succeed without the fluff. My style combines technical style expertise with straightforward business advice because that's what I deliver. Your style should naturally flow from your deeper purpose.

Now it's time to talk about how to face the fear of being seen, even when it feels uncomfortable.

Step 2: Embrace Visibility (Even If You're Nervous)

Like I said before, there is no need to be afraid.

Here are some steps you can take to step into the spotlight with open arms.

Action Steps:
- Start with short-form content (Instagram Stories, TikTok)
- Film one piece of content daily (even if you don't post it)
- Practice talking to the camera for 5 minutes each morning
- Join relevant industry conversations on social media

Mindset Tips:
- Perfectionism kills progress. Done is better than perfect
- Your first 100 pieces of content will be your worst—that's normal
- Focus on helping one person rather than impressing everyone

Building visibility is a slow process, but it becomes achievable with these simple steps. Keep in mind every expert you follow started exactly where you are. The most important element in being the face of your brand is authenticity.

TheSalonGuy® Story

My first videos were terrible. Shaky camera, bad lighting, nervous energy. But I posted anyway. Why? Because waiting for perfection means waiting forever. Those imperfect videos built the foundation of my brand.

Step 3: Be Authentic, Not Perfect

To develop your own voice, follow these steps:

Trust-Building Actions
- Share both successes and failures
- Respond to comments personally
- Show your process, not just results
- Admit mistakes when they happen
- Keep promises to your audience

Content Types to Create
- Not everything has to be scripted; bullet points will work
- Publish actual workplace moments
- Publish actual customer experiences
- Be transparent about product development

Authenticity builds trust, and trust builds brands. But being authentic isn't enough. You need to actively engage with your audience to build real connections. Let's look at how to do that effectively.

Step 4: Engage Like a Human, Not a Brand

Show your *story*, not just the product. To do this, follow these steps:

Daily Engagement Tasks
- Respond to comments within 24 hours
- Answer DMs personally
- Share user content and success stories
- Go live regularly to connect directly
- Ask questions and start conversations

Content Types to Create
- Don't script everything—bullet points work better
- Show real workplace moments
- Share genuine customer experiences

- Be honest about product development

Every time you show up, share your journey and engage with your audience, you build something more valuable than any product or service: trust.

Every video you shoot, every story you tell, and every comment you reply to strengthens that bond. This framework will help you do just that.

Take Action: Be Your Brand

Your brand needs a face.

Your audience needs authenticity.

The only question is: Are you ready to show up?

In the next chapter, we'll cover how to make all of this sustainable. But first, get in front of that camera. Your audience is waiting.

The First 7 Days of Being the Brand Face

- *Day 1-2: Foundation*
    - Create your content guidelines
    - Set up basic filming equipment
    - Film practice content
    - Draft your brand story

- *Day 3-4: Content Creation*
    - Film your first real content
    - Edit and post the first piece
    - Engage with the audience
    - Analyze initial feedback

- *Day 5-7: Engagement*
    - Respond to all comments

- Go live once
- Share behind-the-scenes
- Plan next week's content

Quick-Start Equipment List

Essential Tools:
- Smartphone with good camera
- Basic ring light
- Simple microphone
- Editing app (iMovie/Adobe Rush)
- Content planning app

Chapter 12: Building a Strong HOW

You may have a brilliant HOW in mind. But don't think you are off scot-free just yet.

I've seen a lot of creators with brilliant visions and good plans fail because their execution went wobbly. Not because they weren't talented or hardworking but because they fell into some common traps that derailed their progress.

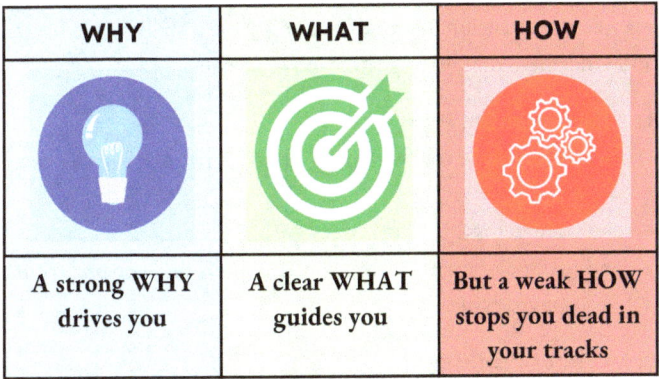

WHY	WHAT	HOW
A strong WHY drives you	A clear WHAT guides you	But a weak HOW stops you dead in your tracks

A Weak HOW Can Be Lethal

A weak HOW is unsustainable. It does not matter how much potential you have because you can't do anything with it.

Here's what happens when your HOW isn't strong enough:

- Your best ideas stay trapped in your head because you lack clear execution steps
- Opportunities slip away because you can't act fast enough
- Your audience loses interest because your delivery is inconsistent
- Resources get wasted on unfocused efforts and false starts
- Motivation drains as you see others passing you by

Each day you run with a weak HOW, you leave money and potential growth behind. Don't let poor execution stand in the way of achieving your goals.

Let's break down the common pitfalls that can sabotage your HOW. And, most importantly, how to avoid them.

Common Expertise Pitfalls to Avoid

These are the real roadblocks that have killed countless promising brands. Pay attention, because avoiding these pitfalls can mean the difference between thriving and barely surviving.

1. **Perfectionism Paralysis**
   - Don't wait for "perfect." Publish, learn, and improve over time
   - Perfect is the enemy of progress
   - Remember: Your first content won't be your best, but it has to exist

2. **Lack of Planning**
   - Failing to plan leads to missed deadlines and inconsistent posting
   - Random action creates random results
   - Without a clear plan, you're just hoping for success

3. **Overcommitting**
   - Don't try to do everything at once. Focus on 1-2 core goals at a time
   - Spreading yourself too thin dilutes your impact
   - Quality suffers when you take on too much

4. **No Review Process**
   - If you're not tracking your progress, you're guessing—not growing
   - What gets measured gets improved

- Regular reviews prevent small issues from becoming big problems

Don't let these traps stand in the way of your momentum. Each is fixable, provided you catch them early and do something about it. Now, on to what might go wrong in scaling your brand.

Common Scaling Mistakes to Avoid

Scaling is where good brands become great... or where they crash and burn. Too many promising entrepreneurs try to scale too fast, too soon, or in the wrong ways.

Here are the mistakes you need to avoid:

1. **Trying to Do Everything Alone**
   - You can't scale without a team or automation tools
   - Lone wolf syndrome leads to burnout
   - Build systems and delegate before you hit your limit

2. **Skipping Quality Control**
   - Don't sacrifice product or content quality to grow faster
   - Growth at the expense of quality is temporary
   - Set clear standards and stick to them

3. **Expanding Too Fast**
   - Scale steadily, not all at once. Test new offerings before going all in
   - Sustainable growth beats rapid explosion
   - Each expansion should build on proven success

4. **Ignoring Health and Wellbeing**
   - Burnout will ruin even the best business. Prioritize rest and balance
   - Your energy is your most valuable resource
   - Schedule downtime like you schedule work

5. **Neglecting Your Core Customer**
   - Stay connected with your core audience as you scale
   - Their loyalty fuels long-term success
   - Growth shouldn't come at the cost of existing relationships

Take your time, build solid foundations, and protect what matters.

Let's move to HOW to stay relevant in a changing market.

Common Scaling Mistakes to Avoid

The market doesn't stand still, and neither should you. But there's a right and wrong way to stay relevant.

Following are some of the mistakes that get your brand to obscurity:

- **Ignoring Trends Completely**
  - Staying disconnected makes your brand outdated
  - Industry changes happen whether you acknowledge them or not
  - Keep one eye on the horizon while staying true to your core

- **Chasing Every Trend**
  - Jumping on every trend dilutes your brand's identity
  - Not every trend deserves your attention
  - Choose trends that align with your WHY

- **Neglecting Core Customers**
  - Never focus on attracting new customers at the expense of existing ones
  - Your loyal following is your foundation
  - Growth should enhance, not replace, current relationships

- **Being Resistant to Change**
  - Refusing to adapt leads to irrelevance

- Change is inevitable; growth is optional
- Adapt without losing your essence

- **Staying Silent**
  - Consistent communication keeps your brand top of mind
  - Silence breeds uncertainty
  - Regular engagement builds trust

Staying relevant means smart adaptation while staying true to your core mission.

TheSalonGuy® Story

When I started scaling my business, I made plenty of mistakes. I tried to do everything myself, from filming to editing to customer service. I worked 18-hour days because that's what I thought scaling meant. And then I hit the wall. My content started to dip, my health suffered, and my audience knew something was up.

That's when it hit me: scaling isn't about working harder; it's about working smarter. I began building systems, delegating tasks, and focusing on what I do best. My business now runs smoother than ever, not because I work more but because I have finally learned how to execute, scale, and stay relevant the right way.

Now that you understand the pitfalls and mistakes that can weaken your HOW let's focus on making it bulletproof.

Building a Stronger HOW

Think of your HOW as a machine. Each part needs to work smoothly with the others. When one part fails, the whole system suffers. But when everything's aligned and running well, your brand becomes unstoppable.

STRATEGIC SYSTEMS ROADMAP

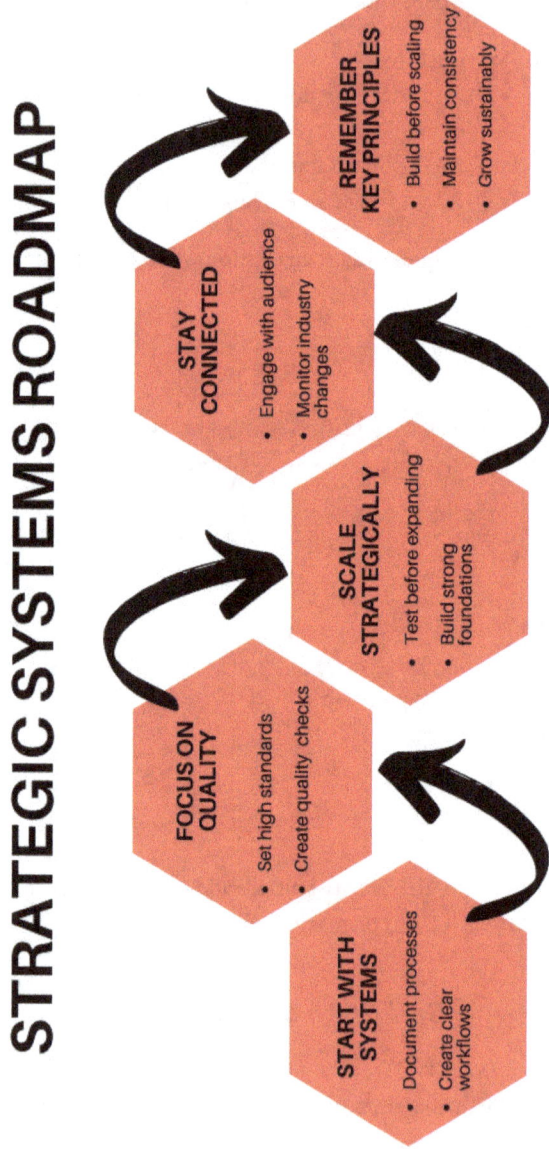

REMEMBER KEY PRINCIPLES
- Build before scaling
- Maintain consistency
- Grow sustainably

STAY CONNECTED
- Engage with audience
- Monitor industry changes

SCALE STRATEGICALLY
- Test before expanding
- Build strong foundations

FOCUS ON QUALITY
- Set high standards
- Create quality checks

START WITH SYSTEMS
- Document processes
- Create clear workflows

Your HOW is your execution engine. It's what separates dreamers from doers, planners from achievers. By strengthening each component (your systems, standards, growth plan, and connection strategy), you create a foundation that can weather any storm and seize any opportunity.

Take Action: Strengthen Your HOW

A strong HOW turns your purpose and plans into reality.

Don't let poor execution derail your success.

Your HOW needs to be as strong as your WHY and WHAT. Take these steps to build a foundation that lasts:

Audit Your Systems
- Review current workflows
- Identify bottlenecks
- Document processes

Create Your Quality Standards
- Define what "good" looks like
- Set clear metrics
- Establish review processes

Build Your Growth Plan
- Set realistic timelines
- Define success metrics
- Plan resource needs

Design Your Connection Strategy
- Schedule regular engagement
- Plan content calendar
- Set communication standards

Zero to Launch:
Get Your HOW Going

You've got your strategy. Now, let's build the machine that makes it work. This blueprint explains exactly HOW to create systems that scale, starting with a five-day sprint to set up your core operations. Instead of taking random action, we're building a foundation that can handle growth.

This isn't about working harder; it's about working smarter. Every hour you invest in these systems saves you ten hours down the road. Let's turn your brand into a well-oiled machine.

System & Scaling Blueprint
5-Day Systems Setup Sprint
Days 1-2: Content Production System   • Setup content calendar and templates   • Create standard operating procedures (SOPs)
Days 3-4: Automation Setup   • Configure scheduling tools and workflows   • Setup email sequences and customer flows
Day 5: Analytics Dashboard   • Setup tracking and reporting systems   • Create a weekly review template
90-Day Growth Milestones
Month 1: Systems and Consistency   • Publish consistently   • Establish routines

| **Month 2: Delegation and Scale** |
| - Hire first team member |
| - Document processes |

| **Month 3: Optimization** |
| - Analyze data |
| - Improve systems |
| - Final review to assess and adjust the growth plan |

The systems you've just built are your competitive advantage. While others are drowning in chaos, you'll have clear processes driving your growth. Start with the 5-day sprint, then use the 90-day milestones to keep you on track.

Remember to protect your power hours. They're the engine of your progress. Visit the detailed chapters for deeper guidance but keep this blueprint handy as your daily reference.

Your systems determine your success. Build them strong from the start.

Conclusion: Take Action Now

Remember how we started? I told you this wouldn't be another fluffy business book collecting dust on your shelf. I promised tactical, practical steps to build your brand. No 18-page childhood stories, no 46-page grammar school memories... just the essential blueprint.

Congratulations!

You've just completed the most straightforward, no-nonsense guide to building a powerful brand.

You now understand:

- WHY you need a clear purpose behind your brand
- WHAT you'll offer through your unique expertise and value-driven content
- HOW to execute, scale, market, and put yourself out there

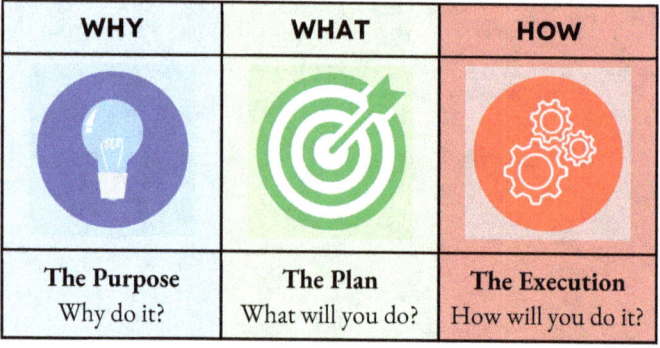

WHY	WHAT	HOW
The Purpose Why do it?	**The Plan** What will you do?	**The Execution** How will you do it?

As you now know, knowledge without action is worthless. The only thing standing between where you are now and where you want to be is execution.

Think back to me walking those 20 blocks in Manhattan, soaked, camera equipment in hand, wondering if it was all worth it. The difference between success and failure wasn't knowledge... it was action. I showed up, even when it was difficult. Even when it seemed crazy. Even when nobody was watching.

Don't wait for the "perfect time" or the "perfect idea." Start today, even if it's just filming your first video or writing your first blog post. Every expert you admire once felt uncertain, but they showed up anyway.

Remember These Core Lessons

1. **Purpose First**
   - Always connect your brand to a meaningful WHY
   - Let your purpose guide every decision
   - Stay true to your mission, even when it's difficult

2. **Value Over Sales**
   - Build trust by helping, educating, and inspiring first
   - Give away your best advice
   - Focus on solving problems, not just making money

3. **Show Up Boldly**
   - Don't be afraid to put yourself out there
   - You ARE your brand
   - Authenticity beats perfection

4. **Execute Relentlessly**
   - Action beats perfection every time
   - Consistency over intensity
   - Keep showing up, especially when it's hard

5. **Adapt and Improve**
   - Stay relevant by evolving with your audience
   - Listen to feedback
   - Keep learning and growing

Your Next Step

Write down three things you will do this week to push your brand forward. Don't just read this book... APPLY it!

Whether it's:

- Launching a product
- Creating a piece of content
- Pitching a collaboration
- Building a system
- Recording a video

Take action today. Not tomorrow. Not next week. *Today.*

10-Day Brand Challenge

"Don't just read this book—ACT on it. Here's your 10-day plan to start building your brand TODAY."

✅ Day 1: Write your WHY statement.

✅ Day 2: Define your core audience.

✅ Day 3: List 3 problems your brand solves.

✅ Day 4: Draft 5 content ideas.

✅ Day 5: Film your first video or post your first blog.

✅ Day 6: Set up your social media strategy.

✅ Day 7: Create a simple product or service offering.

✅ Day 8: Engage with 10 potential followers/customers.

✅ Day 9: Analyze what's working and refine your approach.

✅ Day 10: Commit to consistency—set your next 30-day plan.

Final Thoughts

I started TheSalonGuy® during one of the hardest times in my life, while my mother was ill. I took her strength and used it as fuel. "Failure is not an option" became my way of life.

Your road will not be easy, but it will be worth it. Never stop believing in your brand's potential.

You have everything you could possibly want. Now, create something amazing.

FOLLOW

Follow @thesalonguy on all social media platforms

To purchase hair care products on Shopify:
shop.thesalonguy.com

To purchase courses: courses.thesalonguy.com

YouTube: youtube.com/thesalonguy

Thank you for reading!

Stay inspired, stay driven, and remember:
WHY, WHAT, HOW.

Everything else will follow.